MAKING SPEECHES

Grade 4

By
Shirley C. Granahan

Published by Instructional Fair • TS Denison
an imprint of

Author: Shirley C. Granahan
Editors: Kathryn Wheeler, Sara Bierling

Children's Publishing

Published by Instructional Fair • TS Denison
An imprint of McGraw-Hill Children's Publishing
Copyright © 2003 McGraw-Hill Children's Publishing

All Rights Reserved • Printed in the United States of America

Limited Reproduction Permission: Permission to duplicate these materials is limited to the person for whom they are purchased. Reproduction for an entire school or school district is unlawful and strictly prohibited.

Send all inquiries to:
McGraw-Hill Children's Publishing
3195 Wilson Drive NW
Grand Rapids, Michigan 49544

Making Speeches—grade 4
ISBN: 0-7424-1844-8

1 2 3 4 5 6 7 8 9 MAL 08 07 06 05 04 03

Table of Contents

Note to the Teacher 4
Who's a Speechmaker? 5
Know the Event 6
Know Your Audience 7
Choosing a Topic 8
Kinds of Speeches 9
A Speech to Demonstrate 10-11
A Speech to Inform 12-13
A Speech to Persuade 14-15
A Speech to Entertain 16-17
Research 18
Making Notes and Cue Cards 19
Outlining 20-21
Grammar Check 22-23
The Speech: Opening 24-25
The Speech: Body 26-27
The Speech: Conclusion 28-29
Read and Revise 30
Using Visual Aids 31
Delivery: Voice 32

Delivery: Body Language 33
Practice and Check 34
Nerves: Good News or Bad? .35
Examine a Speech 36-37
Interview and Introduce 38-39
A Presentation Speech 40
Making a School Announcement . . .41
Give a Review 42
Show and Tell 43
Entertain Me! 44
Persuade Me! 45
Answer Key 46-47
Making Speeches Scoring Rubric 48

Note to the Teacher

As educators, we know that students need to practice their oral communication skills. But creating good speechwriters and speechmakers requires a step-by-step process in order to lay a foundation for this crucial skill. *Making Speeches* was designed to help teachers get students on track by combining writing and public speaking skills.

Making Speeches teaches students about the basic types of speeches and the step-by-step process for planning, writing, and delivering them. Students discover that how they look and sound when making a speech is just as important as how they write it. A well-written speech is worthless if no one is interested enough to listen! Activities in *Making Speeches* provide opportunities for students to critique speeches as well as to write and give speeches.

The exercises help students review the requirements of any writing process—proper punctuation, complete sentences, topic or main idea statements, and details to support the main idea. Students also explore the use of descriptive and persuasive words to capture the audience's attention, get the message across, and/or change the audience's point of view.

The speech-writing activities in *Making Speeches* permit young writers to generate their own ideas and practice working with those ideas. Variety of choice is encouraged. Standard exercises also help students strengthen comprehension and critical-thinking skills.

Time and patience are necessary in order to develop good speech-writing and speaking skills. Students need to build self-confidence in their ability to choose topics, put their ideas into words, and get those ideas across in presentations. Some students may have difficulty letting go of their need to read what they wrote rather than speaking naturally using a minimum of notes. *Making Speeches* can help students gain confidence as public speakers who know what they want to say and say it.

Who's a Speechmaker?

Do you give speeches? If you answered "yes," you're right. You give a speech any time you talk and others listen.

You give a speech when you talk about your trip to the Grand Canyon. You give a speech when you try to convince friends to watch a TV show. You give a speech when you tell a group of younger children why they shouldn't play with matches.

Those speeches are called *impromptu* speeches, speeches that are unrehearsed and given on the spur of the moment. There are also *planned* speeches, which are rehearsed. You need to take certain steps to go from giving your daily "speeches" to learning how to plan and rehearse formal speeches.

To write a planned speech, you need to know:
- the event or occasion for the speech.
- who your audience will be.
- the topic of the speech.
- the kind of speech you want to give.

Read each part of a speech about sand. Write **I** (for impromptu) in front of the selection if you think it was unrehearsed. Write **P** (for planned) if you think it was rehearsed. How can you tell?

1. _____ Sand dunes are created when sand is carried by the wind and piled up in hills. Some dunes have piles of sand 1,000 feet deep. For every sand dune that's growing, another is getting smaller. Why? The wind is moving sand from one dune to the next.

2. _____ Last summer we spent a lot of time at the beach. We were interested in watching the wind pile up sand into dunes. That's what they call piles of sand. Anyway, we were told that one dune was almost 50 feet tall! That's a lot of sand for making castles.

3. _____ A park in Indiana is called Indiana Dunes State Park. It's near Lake Michigan. There are some pretty big dunes there. The wind blows across the water and piles up the sand. People even ski on the dunes when it snows.

4. _____ Some sand dunes are short. That's because rocks or tall grass blocks the wind from carrying the sand any farther. The sand piles up against the rocks or grass. But in wide-open areas, dunes often look like ancient pyramids separated by long valleys.

Name _____   Date _____

Know the Event

Why would someone write and make a speech? A speech might be for a formal occasion, such as introducing an important person at a big meeting. Or a speech might be for a casual or informal occasion, such as giving a gift to your grandparents at their fiftieth wedding anniversary party. Different kinds of events set the tone for the different kinds of speeches you might need to make. A casual speech may be impromptu, while a formal speech is often planned beforehand.

Read each part of a speech below. Write **F** in the blank if you think the speech was for a formal occasion. Write **C** if you think the speech was for a casual occasion.

1. ____ Ladies and gentlemen, may I have your attention? I'd like to introduce a writer who really needs no introduction. We all know how her "Harry Potter" books took the world by storm. But what you may not know is that J.K. Rowling is a mother who wrote her first book while her child took naps. Here to tell you more about herself is J.K. Rowling.

2. ____ Thank you. This is a real surprise! I want to thank all of you for the wonderful gift. I thought I was coming to a club meeting. I never guessed there'd be a party for me! I'm going to miss you all when I move away. Thanks again.

3. ____ My fellow Americans, we have all seen stories on the evening news about the increase of crime in our community. But what's being done to protect our homes? What can we do to stop the violence? I have a few ideas I'd like to share with you tonight.

4. ____ I'd like to thank all of you fourth graders for making our booth at the school carnival such a success. We raised over $100 for charity! I heard lots of people talking about how colorful the booth was. Bernie, your idea for the Magic Wheel was a real winner. Great work, team!

5. ____ Many years ago I dreamed of being an actor. I knew if I worked hard enough, I could make it. And tonight is the fulfillment of all my dreams. To have movie fans praise your work is fantastic. But to have other actors praise your work...that's the best.

Name _____ Date _____

Know Your Audience

When you give a speech in class, the audience will be other students. But what if you must give a speech to people you don't know? Some audiences may be made up of people younger than you. Other audiences may be made up of people a lot older. Suppose you plan to talk about chess. What would you tell people who play as well as or better than you? How would you change your speech for an audience who has never played chess? Each speech should have enough interesting and useful information to meet the needs of your audience.

Circle the correct answer.

1. Who would probably be most interested in hearing a speech called "Power Moves in Chess"?
    a. cooking club members
    b. chess club members
    c. gardening club members
    d. all of the above

2. The people most likely to enjoy a speech about car repairs would be—
    a. first graders.
    b. new mothers.
    c. mystery writers.
    d. none of the above

3. Who would be the audience for a speech about why you should be allowed to stay up later on school nights?
    a. your parents
    b. your teacher
    c. your little brother
    d. the neighbor next door

Write your answers on the lines below.

4. List three audiences you think would be interested in a speech called "The Ins and Outs of Inline Skating."
    a. _____
    _____
    b. _____
    _____
    c. _____
    _____

Name _____ Date _____

Choosing a Topic

When choosing a topic, try to pick something that interests you. That way you can make your speech interesting for others. Be sure to pick a topic you can cover in a short speech. For example, you probably wouldn't want to pick "the history of television" as a topic. That's too big a subject and you'd have to talk for hours to cover everything. But you could give a shorter speech called "Television Cowboys of the 1950s."

As you think about topics for a speech, ask yourself these questions.
- Is this topic something that interests me?
- Do I know enough or can I find out enough about the topic?
- Will the audience be interested in hearing about it?
- Can I cover the topic in the time allowed?

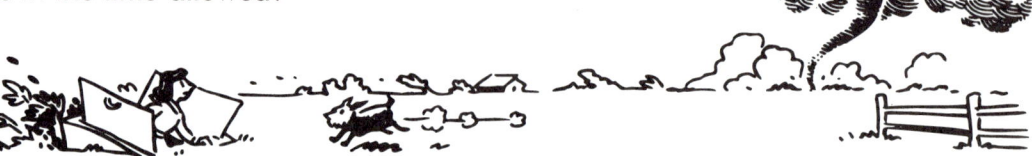

After you pick a topic, you should write the main idea statement. That's the message you want to get across to your audience. Here are a few main idea statements written by students. Write the topic of each speech.

Topic   **Main Idea Statement**

1. _____ People are responsible for pollution, so people should clean it up.
2. _____ Use a standard unit of measurement to find out how long or short something is.
3. _____ The clarinet, a reed instrument, is part of an orchestra's woodwind family.

Now write a main idea statement for each topic listed.

Topic   **Main Idea Statement**

4. Tornadoes _____

5. Vegetarians _____

6. Movie Ratings _____

7. Fossils _____

Name _____ Date _____

Kinds of Speeches

What kind of speech do you want to give? There are four basic types.

Speeches are given to:
- **demonstrate**—discuss a step-by-step process and show the audience how to do something.
- **inform**—give information to help the audience learn about something.
- **persuade**—get people to do something or to change their way of thinking.
- **entertain**—get the audience to laugh.

After you decide what kind of speech to give, write your *purpose* in a statement. This planning statement helps you focus on your goal for the speech. Here are examples.
- I will demonstrate to the audience how to tap dance.
- I will inform the audience about scuba diving.
- I will persuade the audience to raise money for the animal shelter.
- I will entertain the audience with a story about my first skiing trip.

Some speeches use a combination of several basic types. For example, here are four purposes Randy had for a speech about juggling.
- I will demonstrate to the audience how to juggle.
- I will inform the audience about the history of juggling.
- I will persuade the audience to join my new juggling club.
- I will entertain the audience by making some juggling mistakes on purpose.

Now pick a topic you might use for each different kind of speech. You don't have to use these topics later, but you can.

1. I could demonstrate to an audience how to
 .

2. I could inform an audience about _____.

3. I could persuade an audience to _____.

4. I could entertain an audience by _____.

Name _____ Date _____

A Speech to Demonstrate

Are you a good basketball player? Do you cook? Are you great at math? Think of something you do really well. There are lots of topics you can use for a demonstration speech.

Below are a few other topics that students suggested. Circle four ideas you think would make interesting speeches.

how to weave a basket	how to make pizza
how to identify leaves	how to wax a surfboard
how to make a pinwheel	how to put up a tent
how to make spaghetti	how to weave
how to play the flute	how to write an e-mail
how to write haiku	how to putt in golf
how to change the batteries in a flashlight	how to make a picture graph
how to use scuba gear	how to make a hot fudge sundae
how to play a video game	how to wash dishes

In a good demonstration speech, you give step-by-step directions for doing an activity. The directions must be clear and easy to understand. They must also be in the correct order. For example, you can't put icing on a cake until you've mixed the batter and baked it.

1. Maggie is planning to give a demonstration speech about making a peanut butter and jelly sandwich. But she's written the steps out of order. Number the steps in the correct order from 1 to 8 so the demonstration makes sense.

___ Eat and enjoy!

___ Put the jelly-covered bread face down on the peanut-butter slice.

___ Get a plate, a knife, peanut butter, jelly, and bread.

___ Place two slices of bread side-by-side on the plate.

___ Spread jelly on the other slice of bread.

___ Open the peanut butter and jelly jars.

___ Cut the sandwich in half.

___ Spread peanut butter on one slice of bread.

Name _____ Date _____

A Speech to Demonstrate (cont.)

Read each set of step-by-step directions below. Then write the topic of the demonstration speech.

2. Topic: _____

1. Get several slices of bread.
2. Put the bread into the toaster.
3. Set the control for "darker" or "lighter."
4. Push down the lever.
5. Wait until the bread pops up.
6. Carefully take the bread from the toaster— it will be hot.
7. Get a knife and butter, jam, or jelly.
8. Spread butter, jam, or jelly on the toast.
9. Cut each slice in half.
10. Eat.

3. Topic: _____

1. Put dark-colored clothes in one pile and light-colored clothes in another pile.
2. Put detergent and the light-colored clothes into the machine.
3. Set the temperature control and turn on the machine.
4. Take the clothes out when the machine stops and put them into the dryer.
5. Set the temperature control and turn on the dryer.
6. Put detergent and the dark-colored clothes into the washer.
7. Set the temperature control and turn on the machine
8. Take the light-colored clothes from the dryer and fold neatly.
9. Take the dark-colored clothes from the washing machine and put them into the dryer.
10. Set the temperature control and turn on the dryer.
11. Take the dark-colored clothes from the dryer and fold neatly.

4. Think of a topic you might use for a speech to demonstrate. Write the first sentence of that speech.

Topic: _____

First sentence: _____

_____

Name _____ Date _____

A Speech to Inform

> A speech to inform teaches an audience something. Unlike a speech to demonstrate, you don't have to show people how to do something, although you can include a brief demonstration as part of your speech.

Here are a few topics that fourth graders suggested for informative speeches. Do you see any topics for which the speaker might want to include a demonstration in his or her speech to help inform the audience? Circle the four topics you think are the most interesting.

rockets	computer games	bats
digital cameras	minivans	pandas
Martin Luther King, Jr.	soccer	baseball cards
cross-country skiing	laptop computers	mustangs
mysteries	vampires	origami
cartoon animation	wolves	first aid
riverboats	starfish	steam engines

The job of a good reporter is to inform the public. So reporters use the 5Ws (plus an H!) to gather facts that answer the questions: **Who? What? When? Where? Why?** plus **How?**

Read this short speech. Then answer the questions.

   Today people fly back and forth across the ocean every day. Sometimes they travel in big airplanes with lots of passengers. But sometimes they go solo, or travel alone. Think what it must have been like in 1927 for the very first person to fly solo across the Atlantic Ocean. His name was Charles A. Lindbergh. People called him "Lucky Lindy." He wanted to be the first person to fly alone from New York to Paris. His plan was to fly without stopping to get more fuel. He left New York on May 20, 1927, on a small plane named *The Spirit of St. Louis*.
   To fly to Europe in such a small plane, with its small gas tank, Lindbergh had to keep the plane as light as possible. All he took with him were a few sandwiches, a quart of water, and some maps. To save weight, he didn't even take a radio. Imagine Lindbergh, up in his plane all alone. On the ground, the whole world was holding its breath, waiting to hear whether he made it. Finally, after more than 33 hours, word arrived: Lucky Lindy had landed safely outside Paris, France. He was over 3,500 miles away from the field where he took off! Today when people take an airplane ride across an ocean, they should say "thank you" to Charles Lindbergh.

Name _____ Date _____

A Speech to Inform (cont.)

Answer the questions about the speech on page 12.

1. **Who** was the first person to fly solo across the Atlantic? _____
2. **What** was the name of his plane? _____
3. **When** did he fly across the Atlantic? _____
4. **Where** did his plane land? _____
5. **Why** did he make the flight? _____
   _____
6. **How** did he keep the weight on the plane as light as possible? _____
   _____

In a speech to inform, you want the audience to see, hear, smell, and feel what you're describing. For example, the writer said the world was "holding its breath" while waiting to hear about Lindy. You can feel the anxiety, can't you? When you give a speech to inform, use words to help the audience hear the sound of a jet, see a cloud, feel the desert heat, taste the pizza, or smell the aroma of a freshly baked pie.

Read the following parts from speeches. Underline words or phrases that will help the audience's imagination by using one of the five senses.

7. Last summer I visited my grandfather's farm. When I got there, Grandpa wasn't in the old white farmhouse. I stood on the porch and listened. I didn't hear the chug of Grandpa's old tractor, so I knew he wasn't out in the fields. Then I saw Shep, Grandpa's dog, run onto the porch. With his cold, wet nose, Shep nudged me toward the barn. Sure enough, Grandpa was inside, milking the cows while they chewed their sweet-smelling hay.

8. Did you know that nonsmokers can get cancer from tobacco? Cancer is caused by secondhand smoke. That's the thick, smelly cloud above a smoker's burning cigarette, cigar, or pipe. This smoke can make you cough and gasp for air. Secondhand smoke is especially dangerous for small children, senior citizens, and anyone who has a breathing problem such as asthma.

9. Do you like rhubarb pie? I do. My aunt grows rhubarb plants in her garden. The bright green or red stalks grow two-and-a-half feet up from their underground stems. These long, juicy stalks have a bitter taste. You cook them with sugar, which sweetens them up, and use them in pies and jams. But beware! Don't try to eat a rhubarb's large heart-shaped leaves. They contain a poison that can make you ill if you eat them.

Name _____   Date _____

A Speech to Persuade

You give a speech to persuade when you want to change people's minds or get them to do something. You may want neighbors to buy cookies you are selling to raise money for your school. You may want to change people's minds about the school dress code. Or you may want people to get out and vote in the next election. In a persuasive speech, you give your *position*, or point of view. Then you use facts to convince people to do what you want.

A *debate* is a special kind of speech to persuade. In a debate, two people make speeches. One speaker is "for" the idea of the topic, and the other is "against." A debater may not personally agree with the point of view he or she is given. And the audience may agree more with one speaker than the other.

Here are some topics that students chose for their speeches to persuade. Are there really two sides to each topic? Circle the four topics you find the most interesting.

no homework during holidays	change the movie ratings	change the dress code
school lunch menus	surfing the Internet	violence on the news
allow snacks in fourth grade	no detention program	helping the homeless
standardized tests	school safety patrol	hall monitors
loud music	women on NFL teams	raising speed limits
lowering the voting age	too many ads on TV	summer school
the right to a messy room	saving tigers	water pollution

Circle the correct answer.

1. A speech to persuade about standardized tests might—
   a. tell the audience how the tests are written.
   b. tell a funny story about a test.
   c. persuade students that tests are helpful.
   d. none of the above

2. A speech to persuade about loud music might—
   a. compare favorite bands.
   b. describe how loud music can hurt your eardrums.
   c. demonstrate a CD player.
   d. none of the above

Name _____ Date _____

A Speech to Persuade (cont.)

Read Philip's speech to persuade. Then answer the questions.

   Election day is next Tuesday. In this country, voting is one of our most important rights. U.S. citizens over the age of 18 can vote, but it wasn't always that way. When our country was first founded, only white men could vote. Slowly, black men and then women won the right to vote too. The voting age was 21 until 1971. Then it was changed to age 18.

   About 150 million American citizens have the right to vote today. But almost one-third of them don't vote. Some people think their one vote doesn't count for very much. What they forget is that they can vote for changes to schools, neighborhoods, taxes, and more. In a close race, every single vote is important. So please, go home and tell all of your family members over 18 to vote next Tuesday. Your future will depend on it!

3. A good title for Philip's speech would be—
   a. "Excuses for Not Voting."
   b. "America's Voting Age."
   c. "The Constitution Gives Rights."
   d. "Get Out and Vote."

4. After hearing the speech, Philip wants the audience to—
   a. work to get 18-year-olds the right to vote.
   b. get family members over 18 to vote.
   c. give money to a political party.
   d. none of the above

5. What is Philip's position in his speech?

   _____
   _____

6. What are three of the main points Philip made in his speech?
   a. _____
   b. _____
   c. _____

7. What argument does Philip make about the importance of voting?

   _____
   _____
   _____

Name _____ Date _____

A Speech to Entertain

A speech to entertain is a lot of fun. But it may also be the hardest speech to give. That's because it is not supposed to inform people about anything. And it is not supposed to persuade them to do anything. It is just meant to *entertain* people so they have a good time. If you hear laughter when you give this kind of speech, you are doing a good job.

One easy part about giving a speech to entertain is finding a topic. Just think of all the funny things that have happened to you, your pets, and your friends. What happened might not have seemed so funny at the time, but when you think about it later, you laugh.

Here are some topics that fourth graders chose for their speeches to entertain. Circle the four you think would make the funniest speeches.

bubblegum in my hair	teaching Dad to rollerblade	leaving the top off the blender
shampooing the cat	late for school—again	wearing two different shoes
the dog eating my homework	the funniest movie I ever saw	my first time on a toboggan
the spider on my back	the really, really hot cocoa	the best elephant jokes
the day I dropped the eggs at the supermarket	scaring my little brother at Halloween	forgetting all my lines during the play
breakfast on Mother's Day	my grand entrance	learning to bowl
toothpaste on the wall	dressing up my hamster	the food fight
the day I forgot my socks	my neighbor playing the trombone	the cat trapped inside the fold-up bed

Answer the questions.

1. What topic could you use for a speech to entertain?

   _____

   _____

2. What is the topic of the funniest speech or story you have ever heard?

   _____

   _____

Name _____ Date _____

A Speech to Entertain (cont.)

Read Angella's speech to entertain her classmates. Then answer the questions.

    I want to tell you about my big striped cat. Her name is Misty. We actually have two cats, Misty and Duster—but Misty rules. Here's what happens every Saturday morning. Misty wants a "people-food" breakfast: eggs and bacon. If I try to ignore her, she yowls until she gets her own plate. When Misty wants milk, I had better pay attention! If I don't, she jumps up on the counter and gets it herself. Before I know it, eggs, bacon scraps, and puddles of milk are everywhere. Then when I'm cleaning up after Misty, she wants her ears scratched. I think she is letting me know that she forgives me for being so unhappy with her. Isn't it great that she is so forgiving? After she gets her ears scratched, Misty trots off to sleep in Dad's chair. Dad hasn't been able to sit in that chair for years. Sometimes Duster tries to sleep there with her, but he never gets much of a nap. Misty takes up most of the chair. Plus, she snores!

3. Angella gave this speech—
   a. to persuade people to get cats.
   b. to make her classmates laugh.
   c. to make herself seem silly.
   d. to teach people about cats.

4. What is one way Angella helped her audience imagine things in her story?
   a. by talking about the bacon scraps on the floor
   b. by talking about how Misty yowls for food
   c. by talking about Misty snoring in the chair
   d. all of the above

5. What do you learn about Misty in the speech?
   a. She is a quiet, obedient pet.
   b. She rules the household with her demands.
   c. She does not get along with Duster.
   d. She does not get along with Angella.

6. What do you think is the funniest detail in Angella's speech?

   _____

   _____

Name _____ Date _____

Research

You have chosen your topic. You have chosen the kind of speech you want to give. Now you must choose what to say. To do that, you need to discover what you know and don't know about your topic. You may know a lot about the subject already. But sometimes you need to look for more information and a few little-known facts to make your speech more interesting. You can research books and magazines at the library or on the Internet. And you can interview people and take notes about what they say.

When you're ready to start your research, making a **KWL** chart helps. The **K** stands for "What I **K**now," the **W** for "What I **W**ant to Know" and the **L** for "What I **L**earned." Christine started the chart below to plan a speech about the U.S. presidency. First, she listed what she knew. Then she listed what she wanted to know. Finally, she looked for the answers.

K	W	L
• The President is elected every four years.	• Who can be President?	• A candidate for President must be a "natural-born" citizen of the U.S., at least 35 years of age, and have lived in the U.S. for at least 14 years.
• The President lives in the White House in Washington, D.C.	• Who was the youngest President?	
• George Washington was the first President.	• Who was the oldest?	•
• Abraham Lincoln was President during the Civil War.	• What does the President do all day?	•
• The President is the leader of the country.	• Why can't a President continue to be President for many years?	• goes to meetings, signs bills, meets the press, and travels
	• Where does the President go in case of danger?	• Presidents can be elected for only two terms.
		•

Answer the questions about Christine's KWL chart.

1. Name three places where Christine can find information about the U.S. presidency.
   _____

2. Where can Christine find who the youngest and oldest Presidents were?
   _____

3. What other fact does Christine want to find? Name a place where she can look for the answer.
   _____

Name _____ Date _____

Making Notes and Cue Cards

As you do your research, take notes. Use index cards. Don't write everything you read. Just jot down important words and phrases to help you remember what you read. Write one fact on each card. Then you can use these notes as "cue cards" during your speech to remind you of the things you want to say.

A word or phrase web can help you organize your cards. Spread your cards out on a table or on the floor. Then arrange the cards into a web. Put a card with the name of the topic in the center. Place the most important details around it. You may change your mind and decide you don't need all the facts you have on your cards. That's okay. Just remove those cards from the web.

Read the paragraph below. Then create a web of notes from the information. Add more circles if you need them.

In 1973, the United States launched its first space station. It was called Skylab. It was 84 feet long. It weighed 82.5 tons, making it the heaviest object ever put into space. A lab was inside for experiments. There were cameras for photographing Earth's surface. Crews of three astronauts stayed on board for up to 84 days. The astronauts were watched by NASA doctors on Earth. Skylab was damaged during its launch. The first astronauts on board had to fix it. In 1979, the space station fell to Earth. Some pieces of the burned-up station fell on Australia.

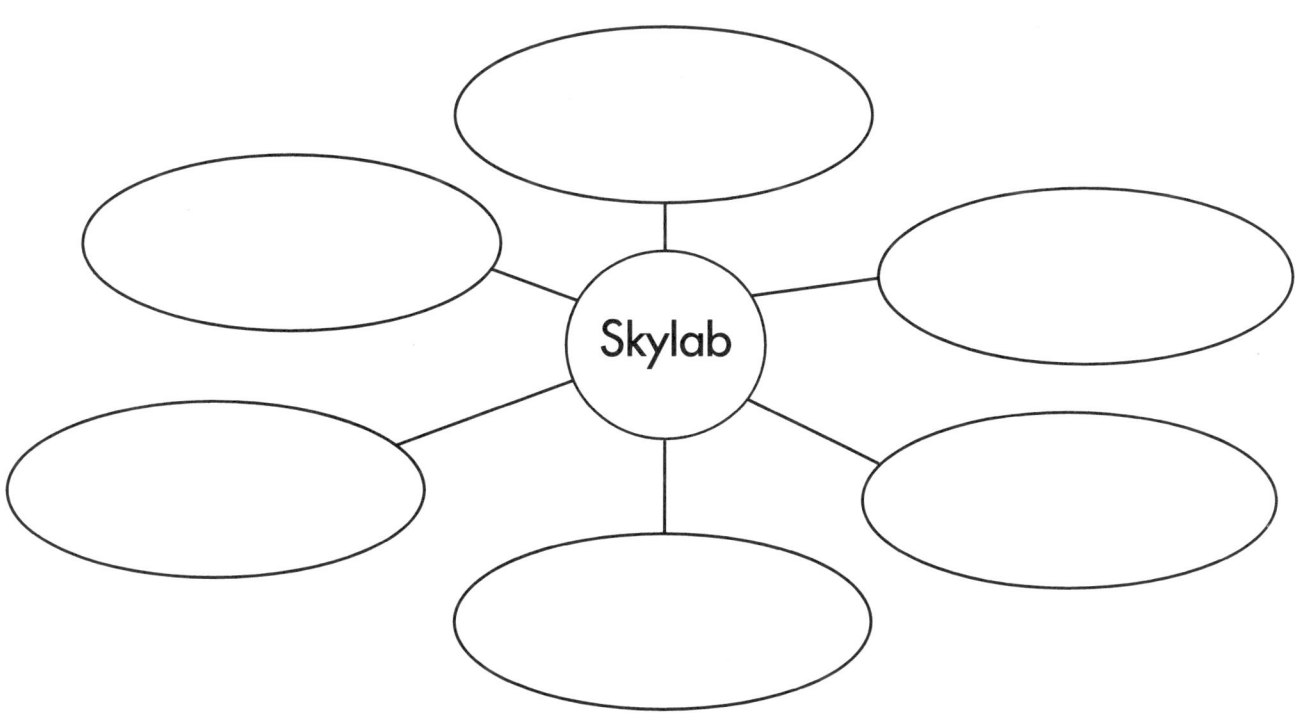

Name _____ Date _____

Outlining

Now that you have the research, are you ready to write your speech? Not yet. It's helpful to make an outline to arrange your ideas. An outline has three parts:

Main Topics: Are labeled A, B, C, and so on. The first word is capitalized.

Subtopics: Are indented to show they relate to the main topic. Are labeled 1, 2, 3, and so on. The first word is capitalized.

Details: Are indented to show they relate to the subtopic. Are labeled a, b, c, and so on. The first word is capitalized.

Read Marta's outline below. Then answer the questions.

          The Olympic Games
A. Ancient Olympic Games
   1. Under the Greeks
      a. When they were held
      b. Where they were held
      c. What games were played
   2. Under the Romans
      a. How they were different
      b. Why they were stopped

B. Modern Olympic Games
   1. When they began
   2. Winter Olympics
      a. When they are held
      b. What events take place
   3. Summer Olympics
      a. When they are held
      b. What events take place
   4. Some modern Olympic stars
      a. From the Winter Olympics
      b. From the Summer Olympics

1. What is the title of the speech?
   _____

2. What are the two main topics?
   _____
   _____

3. What are the four subtopics under topic B?
   _____
   _____
   _____
   _____

4. How many details are listed under subtopic 1 for topic A?
   _____

5. Name one thing you might want to add to this speech.
   _____

© McGraw-Hill Children's Publishing   0-7424-1844-8 *Making Speeches*

Name _____ Date _____

Outlining (cont.)

Neil is planning a speech about clouds. He needs to make an outline. He wants to explain that clouds are made up of water droplets that are formed during the water cycle. The water cycle includes *evaporation*, when water molecules turn into a gas. Next, *condensation* of the gas forms clouds. Finally, *precipitation* falls from the clouds in the form of rain or snow.

Neil also wants to include information about the kinds of clouds that help people know what the weather is going to be. *Cirrus* clouds—high, feathery curls—usually mean rain or snow is coming. *Cumulus* clouds—puffy cotton balls—usually mean good weather. *Stratus* clouds—gray sheets—usually mean rain is coming.

Neil also wants to tell his audience that *alto* means high, *strato* means low, and *nimbus* means rain. These prefixes make longer names for clouds at different heights. An *alto cumulus* cloud is a high, puffy cloud. A *stratocumulus* cloud is a low, puffy cloud. A *nimbostratus* is a gray sheet that holds rain. The lowest clouds of all, at ground level, are called *fog*.

Help Neil by filling in the missing parts of his outline.

Title: _____

A. What clouds are made of
B. _____
　1. Evaporation
　2. Condensation
　3. _____

C. Kinds of clouds
　1. Cirrus
　2. _____
　3. _____
　4. Using clouds to predict _____

D. More about clouds
　1. Heights of clouds
　　a. *Alto* means
　　_____

　　b. *Strato* means
　　_____

　　c. *Nimbus* means
　　_____

　　d. Fog is
　　_____

Name _____ Date _____

Grammar Check

Before you start to write, it's important that you remember some basic grammar rules.

Here are some facts to remember.

- A **sentence** tells a complete idea.
- All sentences begin with a **capital letter**.
- Every sentence has two parts. The **subject**, or *naming part*, tells who or what the sentence is about. The **predicate**, or *telling part*, tells what the subject does, did, or will do.
- A **noun** names a person, place, or thing.
- A **verb** tells what is happening, what has happened, or what will happen.
- A **pronoun** (*he, she, it, you, me, we, them,* or *they*) takes the place of a noun.
- An **adjective** describes a noun.
- An **adverb** tells more about a verb.
- **Prepositions** (*in, on, under, to, from,* and *by*) show place, time, or movement.
- **Conjunctions** (*and, but, or, when,* and *because*) join two words or groups of words.
- The **order of words** in a sentence must make sense.
- Different kinds of sentences have different end marks.

Write the name of each end mark to complete the chart below.

Example	Sentence Kind	End Mark
1. Only birds have feathers.	statement	
2. Did you take my book?	question	
3. Dress warmly.	command	
4. Look out!	command (urgent)	
5. I can't believe I won!	exclamation	

Name _____ Date _____

Grammar Check (cont.)

Put a period, a question mark, or an exclamation mark at the end of each group of words.

6. Are you going to the movies this weekend
7. Leave that alone
8. Please hand me that paper
9. This is my little sister
10. I was so scared

Draw a line between each set of sentence parts.

Subject
11. The mother bear
12. Our VCR
13. Your cousin Sally
14. My new sneakers
15. This meal

Predicate
a. plays on my basketball team.
b. have striped laces.
c. tastes really delicious!
d. has two little cubs.
e. is broken.

Underline each complete sentence.

16. A quill is a kind of bird feather.
17. Where is it?
18. A silly robot.
19. I lost my pencil.
20. In the southwest part of town.

Rewrite each group of words to make sentence sense. Add the correct punctuation.

21. wish I knew I how whistle to

_____

22. music much loud too is That

_____

23. took We train the town into

_____

24. meal most day of Breakfast the important is the

_____

© McGraw-Hill Children's Publishing   0-7424-1844-8 Making Speeches

Name _____ Date _____

The Speech: Opening

Writing a speech isn't all that different from writing anything else. You have something to say, and you want to interest others in learning about it. The main difference is that in a speech, you use as many short, simple sentences as possible. You don't overload the speech with statistics. You want to make everything clear the first time you say it.

As you begin to write a speech, the *opening*, or introduction, is very important. A good opening has two parts. First, you grab the audience's attention. Second, you give the audience a topic sentence that tells in a nutshell what your speech is about. That should make people want to keep listening to find out more. A good opening for a speech should be short, from two to four sentences.

Here are examples of different ways to start a speech. Notice that each example is just two or three sentences.

- **Start with a quote.** *Shakespeare said, "Neither a borrower nor a lender be." But maybe he just didn't understand banking! Today I'm going to tell you why it's okay to borrow from banks.*

- **Start with an interesting number.** *The number 111,111,111 multiplied by 111,111,111 is 12,345,678,987,654,321. Imagine how long it would take to add all those numbers! Today I'm going to talk about the marvels of multiplication.*

- **Start with humor.** *The longest recorded flight of a chicken is 13 seconds. Fortunately, we don't fly on the backs of chickens! Instead, humans invented airplanes so they could stay in the air longer.*

- **Start by linking your speech to another speech the audience has heard.** *Last week Christie told you about some famous baseball players. Today I'm going to tell you more about my favorite baseball player, Babe Ruth.*

Write an example for each of these other ways to start a speech.

1. Start with a simple fact. _____
   _____

2. Start by telling something about yourself. _____
   _____

3. Start with a simple question. _____
   _____

Name _____ Date _____

The Speech: Opening (cont.)

> **Helpful Hints**
> Remember, the opening for a speech:
> - must grab people's attention.
> - has a topic sentence that tells the main idea.
> - should be short, just a few lines.

Now it's your turn. Write an opening for a speech about each topic below. You can use humor, a quote, or one of the options on page 24. Or you can create your own interesting "grabber." Try to write each opening in two or three sentences.

4. watching television _____
_____
_____

5. maps _____
_____
_____

6. pizza _____
_____
_____

7. the solar system _____
_____
_____

8. giving a birthday party _____
_____
_____

© McGraw-Hill Children's Publishing   0-7424-1844-8 Making Speeches

The Speech: Body

> The longest part of a speech is the body, or middle. The body should make up three-fourths of the entire speech. The other fourth is made up of the opening and closing. The body of a speech will have paragraphs to cover all the main topics you planned for your speech. Your speech outline will help you plan this part. Look at the topics, subtopics, and details you listed. Use your notes to help you organize your ideas into a speech. Make sure you put the facts in a logical order. And remember to use short, simple sentences.

Remember this sample opening from page 24? *Last week Christie told you about some famous baseball players. Today I'm going to tell you more about my favorite baseball player, Babe Ruth.*

Read the body of that speech. Underline specific facts used in the body. Notice how each fact is followed by interesting comments.

    George Herman (Babe) Ruth was born in 1895. He had problems with his family. So he ended up living in a home for troubled kids. At the home, one of the teachers talked him into playing baseball. He was so good at the game that he was hired by a team when he was only 19. He was much younger than the other players. So they teased him. They called him the manager's "baby," or "babe." The nickname stuck.

    During his career, Babe Ruth played for Baltimore, Boston, and New York. He played in ten World Series. He could pitch, field, and hit—oh, boy, could he hit! He set the record for 60 home runs in the 1927 season. That record has been beaten now. But no one can take away Babe's honor of being the first player to hit that many homers in a single season. He set other records in runs, batting averages, and slugging percentages. Babe still holds the record for the most bases in a season—457 in 1921.

    Babe was famous for pointing to the area where his next home run hit would go. He'd swing and send the ball flying to the place he had pointed to! He's also remembered for his love of kids. Babe took time to autograph baseballs and to visit kids in hospitals. For his outstanding career as a baseball player, Babe Ruth was voted into the Baseball Hall of Fame.

Name _____   Date _____

The Speech: Body (cont.)

Look back at one of the openings you wrote in the last exercise. In case you forgot, these were the topics: *watching television, maps, pizza, the solar system,* and *giving a birthday party.* Choose one of those topics, picking one you already know something about. You don't need to research the topic first. Just write several short paragraphs about the topic based on what you know right now. Write as if you were talking to somebody. You can choose to inform, persuade, or entertain your audience.

Write your opening here.

_____
_____
_____

Write the rest of your speech here.

_____
_____
_____
_____
_____
_____
_____
_____
_____
_____
_____
_____
_____
_____

_____
_____
_____
_____
_____

Helpful Hint: Keep it simple. A speech should not be too long or too short.

Name _____   Date _____

The Speech: Conclusion

People who come to hear your speech need to know when it's over. To let them know, you summarize the main idea and then wrap up your speech. This two-part ending is called the *conclusion*.

After your quick summary of the main idea, say something to wrap up the speech. You can use humor, a quote, a number, or a fact. Sound familiar? It should, because that's what you did for the opening. The opening sets the tone for your speech. You can link everything together by referring back to your introduction. For example, *If Shakespeare had understood interest rates, he might not have been so frightened of being a borrower—or a lender! I hope you won't be.*

In a persuasive speech, you can let people know the speech is over by asking them to do something. For example, *Please help save the wetlands in our area. Write to your elected officials today.*

Try to wrap up your speech without using phrases such as *in conclusion* or *and finally*. Unless you have just been given an award, don't say *thank you* to end a speech. Remember to keep your ending short. It should be just two or three sentences.

1. Write an ending to this speech to persuade.
   We need Pat Daley as our next class president. Please _____
   _____
   _____
   _____

2. Write an ending to this speech to demonstrate.
   Now you know how to make an origami crane. _____
   _____
   _____
   _____

3. Write an ending to this speech to inform.
   Rail splitter, lawyer, and Civil War President—that was Abraham Lincoln. _____
   _____
   _____
   _____

© McGraw-Hill Children's Publishing   0-7424-1844-8 Making Speeches

Name _____ Date _____

The Speech: Conclusion (cont.)

> **Helpful Hints**
> Remember, the conclusion of a speech:
> - should summarize the main idea.
> - should let the audience know the speech is over.
> - should be only a few lines long.

Reread the opening you wrote on page 25 and the body you wrote on page 27. Now write a conclusion for that speech. First, summarize the main idea of your speech. Then find a way to tie things together and end the speech. Use a question, humor, a number, or any other conclusion you think will work. Did you write a speech to persuade? If so, make sure to end the speech by asking your audience to do something.

Remember to keep the conclusion short. The opening and conclusion together should make up just one-fourth of the speech. When you've finished writing your conclusion, share it with the class.

_____
_____
_____
_____
_____
_____
_____
_____
_____
_____
_____
_____
_____

Helpful Hint: If it fits your topic, end in a way that will leave your audience smiling.

Read and Revise

You have finished writing a speech. Now is the time to look it over for grammar and spelling errors. Then read it aloud to yourself. Does it sound good to you? Use the checklist below to decide if you need to edit and revise your speech.

Speech Checklist

_____ Does my speech tell what I wanted to say?
_____ Is my speech well organized?
_____ Should I add anything?
_____ Should I take anything out?
_____ Could the opening be improved?
_____ Are there interesting facts in the middle?
_____ Should the conclusion be different?
_____ Are there grammar or spelling mistakes?

Read Zhen's speech below. Edit her spelling and grammar mistakes. Would you change anything to make the speech more interesting? Write your suggested changes along the side of the speech or on a separate sheet of paper.

American Cars

In 1908, Henry Ford maid his Model T. Then the the "family car" became common. Before that, cars were expensive. Few peple owned one. It took a long time to make just one car because one worker done all the work. Ford thought it would take less time if the work was divided amonge many workers. And since many cars could be made at the same time, cars would cost lest to make. So Ford installed a assembly line in his factory. Some workers put in engines. Some tighted bolts. Some put on tires. There were many jobs. The work went faster. More people got jobs in the factery! Ford's weigh, known as "mass production," saved time and money. Ford sold his "assembly-line" cars for just $850 each. And he still made a profit. Soon there were thousands of cars in America. America become a motoring nation.

Name _____ Date _____

Using Visual Aids

A *visual aid* is something you bring for an audience to see during your speech. A visual aid can be a graph, a poster, or a photo. It can be a real object or an action you demonstrate. Speakers use visual aids to show how things look, to add information, and to add interest.

Imagine you're going to give a speech about tooth care. Make a list of visual aids you could use. Then write how you would use each one.

Healthy Teeth Visual Aids

1. Aid: _____

   How I would use it: _____

   _____

   _____

   _____

   _____

2. Aid: _____

   How I would use it: _____

   _____

   _____

   _____

3. Aid: _____

   How I would use it: _____

   _____

   _____

   _____

Name _____ Date _____

Delivery: Voice

How you speak is as important as what you say. After all, people must listen to you to get your message. So they should be able to hear and understand you. Your voice is a wonderful tool. You can use it to help people remember the most important parts of your speech. You do that by stressing certain words or facts. All of these things are called *delivery*.

Here is a list of things to remember when speaking to others.

Helpful Hints

- Speak clearly.
- Pronounce your words carefully.
- Use words that everyone can understand.
- Speak slowly enough for people to understand you.
- Vary the speed of your voice so it is not boring.
- Vary the **pitch**—highs and lows—of your voice to stress words.

- Vary the **volume**—loud and soft—of your voice to stress words.
- Try to **project** your voice to the last row. Make sure everyone can hear you, but don't shout.
- Pause to stress a point or to let the audience react.
- Be yourself. Don't try to imitate other speakers. The audience wants to hear what you have to say—in your own way.

Read each sentence aloud. Stress the underlined word. Notice that how you say something can change its meaning.

    <u>Where</u> have you been?

    Where <u>have</u> you been?

    Where have <u>you</u> been?

    Where have you <u>been</u>?

Now read these sentences several times to stress different words. Read each sentence aloud several times. When the sentence sounds the way you want it to, underline the word you are stressing.

1. It's not your turn!
2. Why did you do that?
3. Give that to me!
4. Where did it go?

Name _____ Date _____

Delivery: Body Language

People may speak different languages with their voices. But everyone speaks the same body language. *Body language* is how you stand, use your hands, and use your face. If you look interested in what you're saying, other people will be interested. If you look bored, they will probably be bored too.

Here are some things to remember about body language.

Helpful Hints

- Look from person to person and make eye contact. Each person should think you're talking especially to him or her.
- Smile, unless you're saying something sad or serious.
- Stand up straight. Keep your feet slightly apart.
- Balance your weight on both feet. Don't sway back and forth.
- Keep your hands out of your pockets and off your hips.
- Use your hands for meaningful gestures.
- Try not to fidget.
- Let your personality shine. Don't be afraid to show feelings.
- Don't stop if you make a mistake; just keep going.

You often use body language instead of words. You roll your eyes to show you're bored. You shake your head instead of saying "no." You hold up your hand to vote "yes." You hold out your hands instead of saying "Throw the ball over here!"

Write the body-language movement you would make in these situations.

1. Your friend wants you to go swimming, but the water is freezing. How do you show that it's freezing and you don't want to go in?
   _____
   _____

2. Your friend is walking down the block toward you. How do you tell your friend to hurry up?
   _____

3. You just found out you're moving. How do you show your feelings? _____
   _____

4. Your mother is serving something you don't like for dinner. How can she tell you're not happy about that?
   _____
   _____

© McGraw-Hill Children's Publishing   0-7424-1844-8 *Making Speeches*

Name _____ Date _____

Practice and Check

You've written your speech. You've picked out visual aids. You've got your note cards to cue you about important facts. Now it's time to make the speech. You should practice it at least two times. Practice in front of a mirror or ask a friend to listen to you. If you have a tape recorder, record your speech so you can listen to it yourself. After you've practiced, use the checklist below to figure out how well you did.

Speech Checklist

_____ Did I dress neatly?
_____ Did I dress comfortably?
_____ Did I stand straight and tall?
_____ Did I smile?
_____ Did I speak clearly?
_____ Did I speak loudly enough, but not too loudly?
_____ Did I change my pitch and volume?
_____ Did I use gestures properly?
_____ Did I use clear and useful visual aids?
_____ Did I remember my first and last line?
_____ Did I look at my notes, but not too much?
_____ Did I get the audience's attention?
_____ Did I make good eye contact?
_____ Did I cover all my ideas?
_____ Did I meet my goal to demonstrate, inform, persuade, or entertain?

Write a short answer to each question.

1. What should you do if you forget part of your speech? _____
_____

2. Why should you make eye contact with audience members? _____
_____

3. What is one thing you could do to help you remember when to use your visual aids? _____
_____

Name _____ Date _____

Nerves: Good News or Bad?

If you get nervous before you speak, you're not alone. Even great actors get nervous before they perform. The only people who don't get nervous are people who don't care if they do a good job. Those people who do care may find they have "butterflies in their stomachs" or sweaty hands. They need to relax.

Here are some tips to help you relax before your speech.

- Make sure you've prepared and practiced the speech.
- Wear something comfortable.
- Do some exercise, such as walking or jogging.
- Try deep breathing. Breathe in through your nose. Hold your breath and count to five. Then breathe out through your mouth.
- Close and open your fists.
- Picture yourself doing a good job. Then you probably will.

Here are some tips to help you relax at the start of your speech.

- Relax and take a deep breath.
- Stand up tall.
- Look straight ahead.
- Walk to the spot where you are going to stand.
- Turn and look directly at the audience.
- Smile.

Here are some tips to help you relax during your speech.

- Use index cards to keep yourself organized.
- Don't stand still. Use gestures to help make your points.
- Make eye contact with a friendly face.
- Pause and take a deep breath.
- Think about why you chose the topic—because it interested you!

Write down three things from this page that you think would help you relax the most. Then add one more idea of your own.

1. _____
   _____
   _____

2. _____
   _____
   _____

3. _____
   _____
   _____

4. Your idea: _____
   _____
   _____

© McGraw-Hill Children's Publishing   0-7424-1844-8 Making Speeches

Examine a Speech

Angella wrote a speech about cats. Read what she wrote. Then answer the questions.

I read that cats have over 100 different vocal sounds. Well, I believe it. My cat, Misty, uses every one of those sounds to wake me up in the morning! Sometimes Misty is a pest, but she's a great companion. We got Misty from the animal shelter almost eight years ago. She and I have grown up together. As you can see, she's a gray and white tabby. That's a popular breed of cat.

Did you know that the cat is one of the most popular house pets? As you can see from this chart, experts estimate that in the United States alone, there are more than 60 million cats. But there are millions of other cats who are homeless, roaming the city streets and the countryside. That's why we're raising money today to help our local animal shelter. The shelter needs to build a new addition to its building. Then it can care for more homeless animals. Won't you please help? Or better yet, adopt a cat. I'm sure all the cats will join Misty in saying "thank you," with their 100 vocal sounds!

1. What kind of speech is this?
    a. demonstrative
    b. informative
    c. persuasive
    d. none of the above

2. Angella opens her speech by—
    a. asking a question.
    b. using humor.
    c. using a quote.
    d. using a specific fact.

3. Angella asks the audience to—
    a. give money or adopt a pet.
    b. help dig the foundation for a building.
    c. buy Misty a gift.
    d. vote for her for mayor.

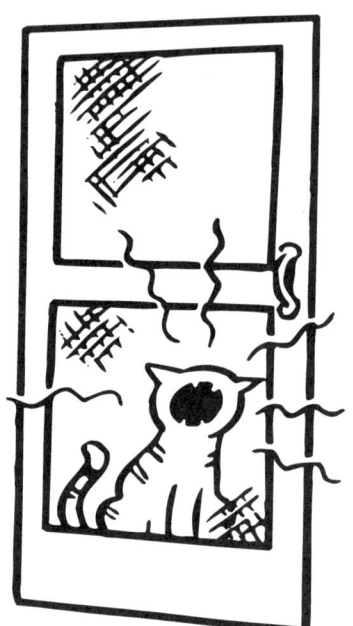

Name _____   Date _____

Examine a Speech (cont.)

Answer the questions about the speech on page 36.

4. What two visual aids do you think Angella used? Write them down. Then copy the sentence in the speech where she used each one.

   Visual Aid 1: _____
   Sentence in speech where it was used:
   _____
   _____

   Visual Aid 2: _____
   Sentence in speech where it was used:
   _____
   _____

5. Which five words or phrases do you think Angella should stress? Write them on the lines.
   a. _____
   b. _____
   c. _____
   d. _____
   e. _____

Now try this. Write a short speech about your pet or about a good cause. Fill in the speech plan below. Use facts to help you organize your speech. Then write your speech on another sheet of paper.

6. What kind of speech will it be?
   _____

7. What is the topic?
   _____

8. What opening will you use to grab everyone's attention?
   _____
   _____
   _____

9. List four things you want people to know about the topic.
   a. _____
   b. _____
   c. _____
   d. _____

10. How will you end your speech?
    _____
    _____
    _____
    _____

© McGraw-Hill Children's Publishing   0-7424-1844-8 Making Speeches

Name _____ Date _____

Interview and Introduce

> One way to get over the fear of speaking in public is to make an introduction. You may choose to interview a classmate, another friend in school, or even a teacher.

Read the questions below and add four more of your own. Write your answers in the chart.

Question	Notes
1. When and where were you born?	
2. Do you have brothers and sisters? If so, how many?	
3. What do you like to do for fun?	
4. What's your favorite color?	
5. What's your favorite TV show?	
6. What's your least favorite food?	
7. What's the most exciting thing that's ever happened to you?	
8. What's the worst thing that's ever happened to you?	
9.	
10.	
11.	
12.	

Use your notes to help you write a short speech about the person you interviewed. Then give the speech to introduce him or her to your classmates. Don't tell the person's name until the end of the speech.

© McGraw-Hill Children's Publishing   0-7424-1844-8 Making Speeches

Name _____ Date _____

Interview and Introduce (cont.)

> Here's a speech Juan wrote about his gym teacher. Juan asked the teacher to stand outside the room until he had finished his introduction.

Where would you go to if you wanted to know about rock climbing? Well, look no further than our school. We have an expert right here! This rock climber comes from a large family. During most summers, the family would go on rock-climbing trips—from Oregon to New Hampshire. They even let their dogs go on rock climbs, if the climbs weren't dangerous.

This person can also answer any question you have about ballet. After all, she says, the trick to climbing over big rocks is balance and grace. Those are the same skills you need for ballet.

Besides rock climbing and dancing, this person likes to ski, jog, and watch TV. Most of her TV time is spent watching cartoons and game shows. "The cartoons bring back memories of all my brothers and sisters and me watching TV on Saturday mornings," she says. "The game shows remind me of when our whole family watched TV in the early evenings." This person also loves kids—and kids seem to love her back. I'd like to present the best gym teacher we know—Mrs. Davis!

Write answers to the questions about Juan's speech.

1. How did Juan grab the audience's attention without using the person's name?
   _____
   _____

2. What were the four most important facts about the person Juan was introducing?
   a. _____
   b. _____
   c. _____
   d. _____

3. How did Juan end his speech?
   _____
   _____

Helpful Hint: Use a pause to stress something in your speech. Juan probably paused after making the connection between rock climbing and ballet.

Name _____ Date _____

A Presentation Speech

A presentation speech is given when someone is being honored with an award. Sometimes the speech is given at public events. Other times it is given at meetings, in school assemblies, or in classrooms.

Use the following facts, plus your imagination, to plan a short speech.

In your club, every member does something to help people in the community. At the end of each year, the person who does the best job is given an award. This year you visited a nursing home once a month. Your best friend, Chris, collected food for the homeless shelter. He spent every weekend there, serving meals and helping to wash dishes. He's been picked to receive the "Good Citizen Medal" and a $50 gift certificate from a local bookstore. The other club members have asked you to give a short speech about Chris at the next club meeting. At the end of your speech, you will give Chris the award.

1. Who will be in your audience?
   _____
   _____

2. What are the main ideas you want to cover in your speech?
   a. _____
   b. _____
   c. _____

3. Write down three people who might give you more information about Chris's work at the shelter.
   a. _____
   b. _____
   c. _____

4. Describe two visual aids you could use in your speech.
   a. _____
   b. _____

5. What should be the last point in your speech? Write the ending.
   _____
   _____

© McGraw-Hill Children's Publishing   0-7424-1844-8 Making Speeches

Name _____ Date _____

Making a School Announcement

Sometimes a school announcement requires a short speech. You may want to inform the school about an upcoming event, a class play, or a new club.

You and a friend want to start a science club at school. You want to call it "Sensational Science." Your fourth-grade teacher, Mr. Hanson, has agreed to be the sponsor. That way you can meet in the school after school hours. You check the after-school schedule and discover that Thursday at 3:45 is the only time available. You look for a room that is big enough for experiments. You find that your club can meet in Room 107, which is a good size. You want kids from any grade to join the club. They can come to the first club meeting to join. Mr. Hanson suggests telling everyone about the club over the PA system during the morning announcements. The school principal says you can make the announcement Monday morning. You will have two minutes to speak. What should be included in your announcement?

Fill in the speech plan below.

1. What kind of club do you want to start? _____

2. What is the name of the club? _____

3. Who can join? _____

4. Who is the sponsor, or adult in charge? _____

5. When will the club meet? (day and time) _____

6. Where will the club meet? (room number) _____

7. How should people let you know that they want to join? _____
   _____

Use the speech plan to write your announcement on another sheet of paper.

© McGraw-Hill Children's Publishing   41   0-7424-1844-8 Making Speeches

Name _____ Date _____

Give a Review

A book report is a speech to inform. You tell others what you did or didn't like about a book and if you think they'd like it. You can also write and give a review of a play, movie, TV show, music concert, or sporting event.

Fill in the book report form below with notes about a book you just read. Fill in the second review form with notes about your favorite TV show. After finishing the forms, choose one to create a speech to give in class. Use the planning form to help you organize your speech.

Book Report

Title of book: _____

Author: _____

Illustrator/Photographer: _____

Main topic of the book: _____

_____

List three facts you learned from the book.

1. _____
   _____
2. _____
   _____
3. _____
   _____

Give reasons why you think others will or won't like the book.

_____
_____
_____
_____

TV Show

Title of TV show: _____

Names of two characters: _____

_____

Kind (such as mystery, comedy, cartoon, adventure, or drama): _____

_____

List three reasons why you like the show.

1. _____
   _____
2. _____
   _____
3. _____
   _____

Give reasons why you think others will or won't like the show.

_____
_____
_____
_____

Name _____ Date _____

Show and Tell

The fourth graders decided to try their speech-making skills on other audiences. Christine gave her U.S. Presidents speech to a fifth-grade class that was studying about the presidency. For visuals, she used a map of Washington, D.C., a chart showing the rooms in the White House, and a poster showing all the U.S. Presidents. Neil gave his cloud speech to several second-grade classes. His visuals included a sequence chart of the water cycle and a poster he made about clouds, using lots of cotton balls. The other classes enjoyed having the fourth graders speak to them. Christine and Neil had fun too.

Plan a speech for another class in your school. You might want to speak to younger students. Or you might want to speak to older students. Check with the other teacher for permission to give your presentation.

Fill in the speech plan.

1. What topic could you choose that would interest younger students?
   _____
   _____

2. What topic could you choose that would interest older students?
   _____
   _____

3. What main ideas do you want to cover?
   a. _____
   b. _____
   c. _____

4. What visual aids will you use?
   a. _____
   b. _____

5. What would you need to change in your speech to present it to a younger or older audience?
   _____
   _____
   _____
   _____
   _____
   _____
   _____
   _____
   _____
   _____
   _____
   _____

Helpful Hint: If you're not sure what topic to pick, ask older or younger friends or relatives about their interests.

Name _____ Date _____

Entertain Me!

> Now it's time to try one of the most challenging speeches: a speech to entertain your audience.

Read the speech to entertain that Raoul gave to his class.

I'll never forget my sixth birthday party. Mom let me invite all my friends. I insisted that my best friend come to the party too—my dog, Dinky. "All right," said Mom. "But you'll have to watch him every minute. You know what he's like."

My friends arrived and we started to play games. I forgot all about Dinky. First, he went to the bedroom where the coats were and chewed some of them. Then he went to the pile of presents and "unwrapped" most of them. His next move was to attack my birthday cake! When it was time to cut the cake, I found a huge hole in it. Dinky had a great time at my party, but nobody else, for some reason, wanted a piece of cake.

Fill in the form below to organize your thoughts. Then write and give a three- to five-minute speech. You'll know you did a good job if you hear laughter.

1. What will be the topic of your speech to entertain?
   _____
   _____

2. What main ideas do you want to cover?
   A. _____
   B. _____
   C. _____

3. What visual aids will you use?
   A. _____
   B. _____

Helpful Hint: Rehearse your speech in front of your family or a friend. Try sound effects and humorous facial expressions to make your story even funnier.

Name _____ Date _____

Persuade Me!

A speech to persuade is one that requires lots of good points for the side or cause you are representing. Remember to end the speech by asking people to do something.

Pick a topic from page 14 or one of those listed below. You can also use an idea of your own.

- Pick an idea that not everyone agrees on. For example: "There should be soda vending machines in the cafeteria." You can be for or against having soda available to those who wish to buy it.
- You are one of three candidates running for president of your activity club. Write a speech telling why you're the best candidate. What would you do for club members if elected? Persuade as many of your classmates as possible to vote for you.
- A lot of accidents have happened on your street because cars go too fast. You want a stoplight installed or the speed limit lowered. You have a chance to speak before your city council next week. Your speech should persuade the council to make your street safer.

Fill in the form below to organize your thoughts. Then write and give a three- to five-minute speech.

1. What will be the topic of your speech to persuade?
   _____
   _____

2. What main ideas do you want to cover?
   a. _____
   _____
   b. _____
   _____
   c. _____
   _____

3. What visual aids will you use?
   a. _____
   b. _____

Helpful Hint: Try picking a topic that has two strong sides. Choose one side to present in your speech. An issue or a rule in your school might be a good choice.

© McGraw-Hill Children's Publishing   0-7424-1844-8 *Making Speeches*

Answer Key

Who's a Speechmaker?..................Page 5
1. P
2. I
3. I
4. P

Know the Event..................Page 6
1. F
2. C
3. F
4. C
5. F

Know Your Audience..................Page 7
1. b
2. d
3. a
4. Examples: elementary students, members of a skating club

Choosing a Topic..................Page 8
1. pollution
2. standard units of measurement
3. clarinets
4. Example: Tornadoes are strong windstorms that swirl around a center and cause many thousands of dollars of damage each year.
5. Example: Some people and animals are vegetarians. They do not eat meat, but get nutrients from plant foods instead.
6. Example: Movies are rated to let people know whether bad words or violence is used in the film.
7. Example: Fossils are the remains or prints of plants and animals that lived long ago. They help us learn about the past.

Kinds of Speeches..................Page 9
1.–4. Answers will vary.

A Speech to Demonstrate..................Pages 10–11
Answers will vary on circled topics.
1. Steps should be numbered 8,6,1,2,5,3,7,4
2. Topic: Making Toast
3. Topic: Washing Clothes or Doing the Laundry
4. Answers will vary.

A Speech to Inform..................Pages 12–13
Answers will vary on circled topics.
1. Charles Lindbergh
2. *The Spirit of St. Louis*
3. 1927
4. Paris or outside Paris
5. He wanted to be the first person to fly across the Atlantic.
6. He took only sandwiches, water, and maps.
7. old white farmhouse; chug of Grandpa's old tractor; his cold, wet nose; sweet-smelling hay
8. thick, smelly cloud; a smoker's burning cigarette, cigar, or pipe; make you cough and gasp for air
9. bright green or red stalks; grow two-and-a-half feet; long, juicy stalks; bitter taste; large heart-shaped leaves

A Speech to Persuade..................Pages 14–15
Answers will vary on circled topics.
1. c
2. b
3. d
4. b
5. Answers will vary. Examples: Voting is an important right. Voting can affect many important issues in a voter's life.
6. Examples: not everyone has had the right to vote; only one-third of eligible voters vote; every vote is important
7. Answers will vary. Philip tells his audience that their future will depend on whether their family members vote.

A Speech to Entertain..................Pages 16–17
Answers will vary on circled topics.
1. Answers will vary.
2. Answers will vary.
3. b
4. d
5. b
6. Answers will vary.

Research..................Page 18
1. Internet, encyclopedia, book about presidential facts
2. in a book about presidential facts and statistics; on the White House Web site
3. Where does the President go in case of danger? She could look at a Web site about the White House or use a search engine.

Making Notes and Cue Cards..................Page 19
Web should be filled in with details from paragraph. The words or phrases will vary but might include: first U.S. space station, launched in 1973, 84 feet long, 82.5 tons, cameras to photograph Earth, lab for experiments, three astronauts at a time, 84 days on board, damaged in launch, fell to Earth in 1979.

Outlining..................Pages 20–21
1. The Olympic Games
2. Ancient Olympic Games and Modern Olympic Games
3. When they began, Winter Olympics, Summer Olympics, Some modern Olympic stars
4. three
5. Answers will vary.
Outline spaces should be filled in as follows:
Title: Answers will vary. Example: All About Clouds
B. Clouds and the water cycle
B. 3. Precipitation
C. 2. Cumulus
C. 3. Stratus
C. 4. weather
D. 1. a. high
D. 1. b. low
D. 1. c. rain
D. 1. d. ground-level clouds

Grammar Check..................Pages 22–23
1. period
2. question mark
3. period
4. exclamation point
5. exclamation point
6. question mark
7. period or exclamation point
8. period
9. period
10. exclamation point
11. d
12. e
13. a
14. b
15. c
16. underlined
17. underlined
18. no underline
19. underlined
20. no underline

Answer Key

21. I wish I knew how to whistle.
22. That music is much too loud.
23. We took the train into town.
24. Breakfast is the most important meal of the day.

The Speech: Opening..................Page 24–25
1. Answers will vary.
2. Answers will vary.
3. Answers will vary.
4. Example: What educates, informs, entertains, and persuades—sometimes all at once? Your television!
5. Example: When Christopher Columbus set out to discover a new world, he would have had an easier trip with a map. Today most of the world is charted, which means maps are available to show the way.
6. Example: Pizza offers lots of variety. It's delicious. It's easy to share. Is pizza the world's most perfect food?
7. Example: Our solar system has eight planets revolving around the sun. But could there be undiscovered planets in our cosmic neighborhood?
8. Example: The day I said I would plan my little sister's birthday party, I must have been insane. Her birthday party was, in fact, the craziest experience of my life!

The Speech: Body ....Pages 26–27
Specific facts in the Babe Ruth speech should be underlined.
Opening and body of speech should be written. Closing will be added later.

The Speech: Conclusion ....Pages 28–29
1. Example: Please cast your vote for Pat this Tuesday, for the good of our whole class!
2. Example: This ancient decoration symbolizes peace, and I hope you find it peaceful to make a beautiful crane of your own.
3. I hope you have enjoyed learning more about one of our most amazing Presidents.

Closing of speech should match and connect with opening and body on pages 25 and 27.

Read and Revise..................Page 30
Corrected Essay:
In 1908, Henry Ford <u>made</u> his Model T. Then (delete extra *the*) the "family car" became common. Before that, cars were expensive. Few <u>people</u> owned one. It took a long time to make just one car because one worker <u>did</u> all the work. Ford thought it would take less time if the work was divided <u>among</u> many workers. And since many cards could be made at the same time, cars would cost <u>less</u> to make. So Ford installed <u>an</u> assembly line in his factory. Some workers put in engines. Some <u>tightened</u> bolts. Some put on tires. There were many jobs. The work went faster. More people got jobs in the <u>factory</u>. Ford's <u>way</u>, known as "mass production," saved time and money. Ford sold his "assembly-line" cars for just $850 each. And he still made a <u>profit</u>. Soon there were <u>thousands</u> of cards in America. America <u>became</u> a motoring nation.
Other Changes—Answers will vary. Accept any revision that makes sense and/or enhances the speech as written.

Using Visual Aids ....Page 31
Answers will vary but might include: toothbrush, toothpaste, dental floss, poster about dental health, model of teeth, posters showing parts of the tooth, X-ray of a tooth, and picture of a dentist checking teeth.

Delivery: Voice ....Page 32
1.–4. Answers will vary.

Delivery: Body Language ....Page 33
1. hug yourself, shiver, shake your head
2. motion toward yourself in a quick pattern

3. Answers will vary depending on how students feel about moving.
4. stick your tongue out, frown, gag

Practice and Check ....Page 34
1. Keep going or move to the next point.
2. It makes each person think you are talking just to him or her.
3. Answers will vary. Example: Make notes in red ink on cue cards for each visual aid.

Nerves: Good News or Bad? ....Page 35
1.–4. Answers will vary.

Examine a Speech ....Pages 36–37
1. c
2. d
3. a
4. Photo of Misty; "As you can see, she's a gray and white tabby."
Chart of popular pets; "As you can see from this chart, experts estimate that in the U.S. alone, there are more than 60 million cats."
5. Answers will vary.
6-10. Answers will vary.

Interview and Introduce ....Page 38–39
1.-12. Answers will vary.
1. by describing the person as an expert on rock climbing
2. loves rock climbing; interested in ballet; TV shows remind her of her time with her family; loves kids
3. by introducing Mrs. Davis, the gym teacher

A Presentation Speech ....Page 40
1. other club members; perhaps Chris's family
2. Examples:
   A. Chris's dedication to his work at the shelter
   B. Chris's specific tasks and Chris's shelter schedule
   C. Presentation of the medal and gift certificate to Chris
3. A. one of his parents
   B. a supervisor at the shelter
   C. other club members
4. A. a photo of Chris at work
   B. a letter from the shelter supervisor
5. Presenting the medal and gift and asking everyone to thank Chris for his outstanding achievements; Endings will vary.

Making a School Announcement ....Page 41
1. a science club
2. Sensational Science
3. any interested student
4. Mr. Hanson
5. Thursdays, 3:45
6. Room 107
7. They should come to the first meeting.

Give a Review ....Page 42
Answers will vary for the book report and the TV show.

Show and Tell ....Page 43
1.–5. Answers will vary depending on the chosen topic.

Entertain Me! ....Page 44
1.–3. Answers will vary depending on the chosen topic.

Persuade Me! ....Page 45
1.–3. Answers will vary depending on the chosen topic.

Making Speeches Scoring Rubric

Use this 5-point rubric to score student performance.
4 = Excellent
3 = Good
2 = Average
1 = Poor
0 = Incomplete or unscorable

Student's Name: _____ **Date:** _____

Basic Speech Type: (circle one)
    Demonstrative   Informative
    Persuasive   Entertaining

Name of Speech _____

SCORE	CRITERIA	ADDITIONAL COMMENTS
	Topic selection: is appropriate for the audience	
	Topic selection: fits the speech type	
	Writing: uses proper sentence structure	
	Writing: uses correct grammar and appropriate language	
	Introduction: gets audience's attention and states purpose	
	Body: is clearly organized and developed	
	Conclusion: wraps up thoughts	
	Delivery: is natural, and indicates self-confidence	
	Delivery: uses appropriate posture, eye contact, gestures, and facial expressions	
	Delivery: uses clear articulation and pronunciation, volume, pitch, and pace	
	Visuals: are appropriate and enhance the presentation	
TOTAL		